Marty Woods is a renowned international artist based in Kuala Lumpur, Malaysia. He is known for his intricate black and white drawing which he refers to as 'intricacies'. He is also a published author with international publisher and has authored Exotic Kingdom An Inspiring Coloring Book, Color The Rainforest An Exotic Coloring Book and Bunian and Hidden Intricacies. His books are sold worldwide and available from all major bookstores.

Marty Woods has been featured in Air Asia Travel 3Sixty in-flight magazine, The Star & New Straits Times(national newspapers), BFM Radio Station, Colorplaner website, Color On Magazine and social news network SAYS. He was voted as Top Doodler in Malaysia by Tally Press in 2016 and has collaborated with major brands such as Starbucks, San Francisco Coffee, Nespresso, Disney Malaysia, Pandora, SMO Bookstores, TM Malaysia, TIME Internet, Swiss Watch Gallery, Shell, WWF, Doodle Malaysia and Creative Volts.

www.hellomartywoods.com
www.facebook.com/hellomartywoods
www.instagram.com/hellomartywoods
www.patreon.com/hellomartywoods
marty.kreativkontentz@gmail.com

Intricate Alphabets
by Marty Woods

Copyright text and illustrations (c) 2018 by Marty Woods. All rights reserved. No part of this publication may be reproduced, stored in a retrieval system, or transmitted in any form or by any means, electronic or mechanical, including photocopy, without permission in writing from the author.

For PDF version, you may print the pages to color over and over again, and share your colored in-progress/finishes on websites or social media, but sharing or redistributing this book, in any digital or printed form, all or in part, is strictly prohibited by copyright law. These images are also not to be used for commercial purposes of any kind, colored or uncolored. Thank you so much for buying this book and supporting independent artist.

Exotic Kingdom An Inspiring Coloring Book ISBN 0373100000, 9780373100002
Color The Rainforest An Exotic Coloring Book ISBN 0373135467, 9780373135462
Bunian and Hidden Intricacies PDF version available on Etsy Store

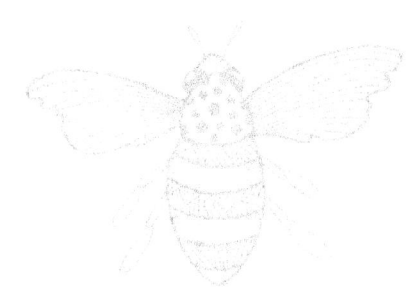

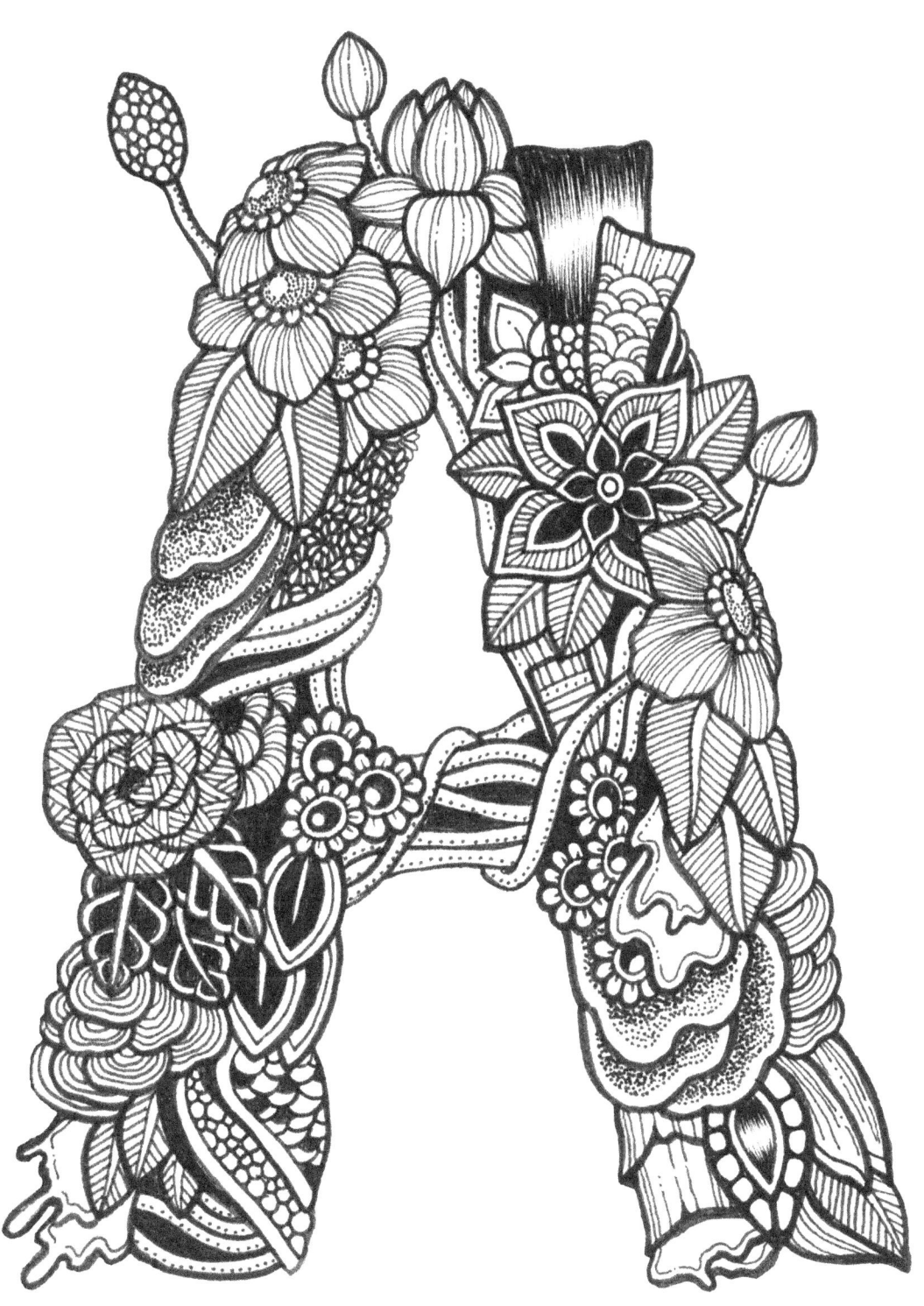

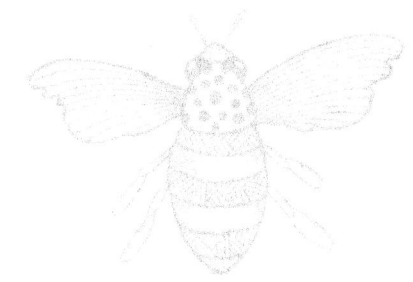

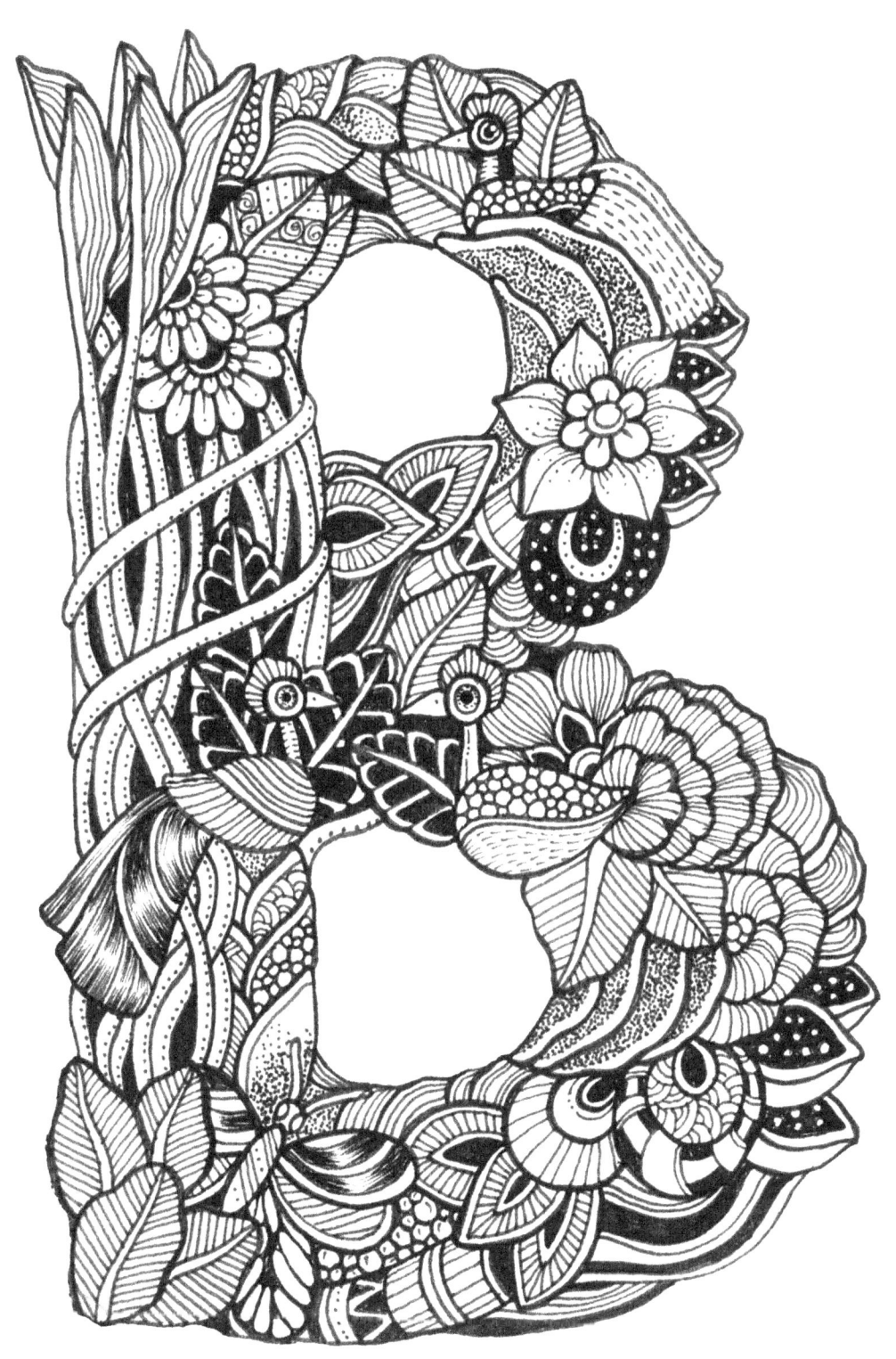

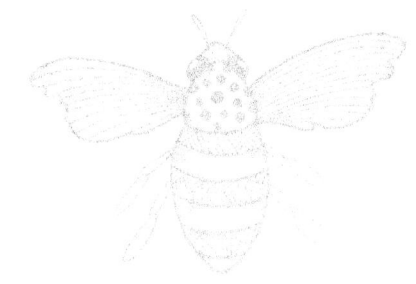

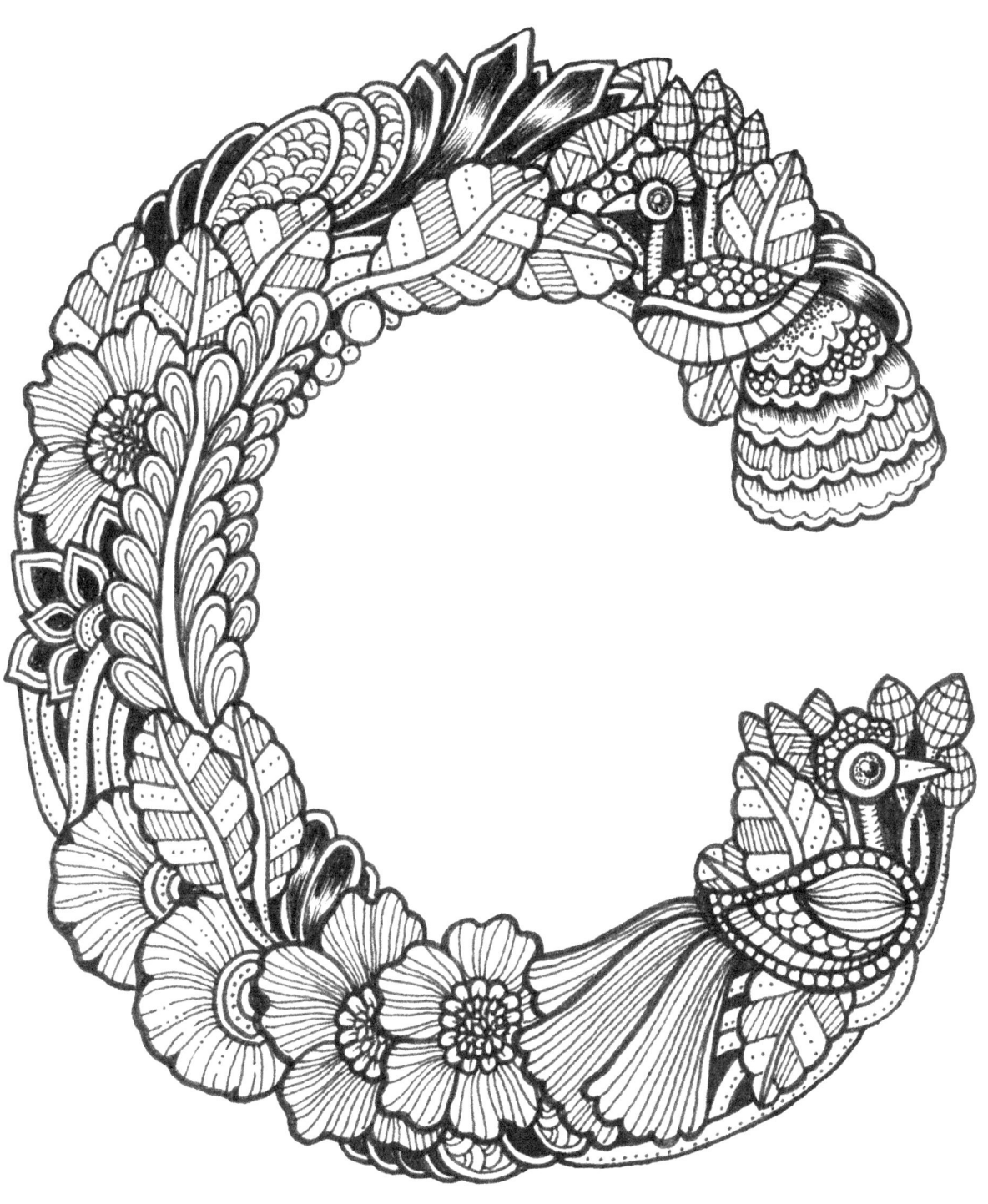

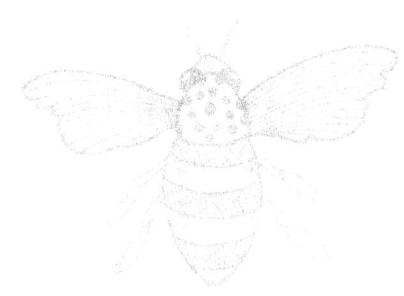

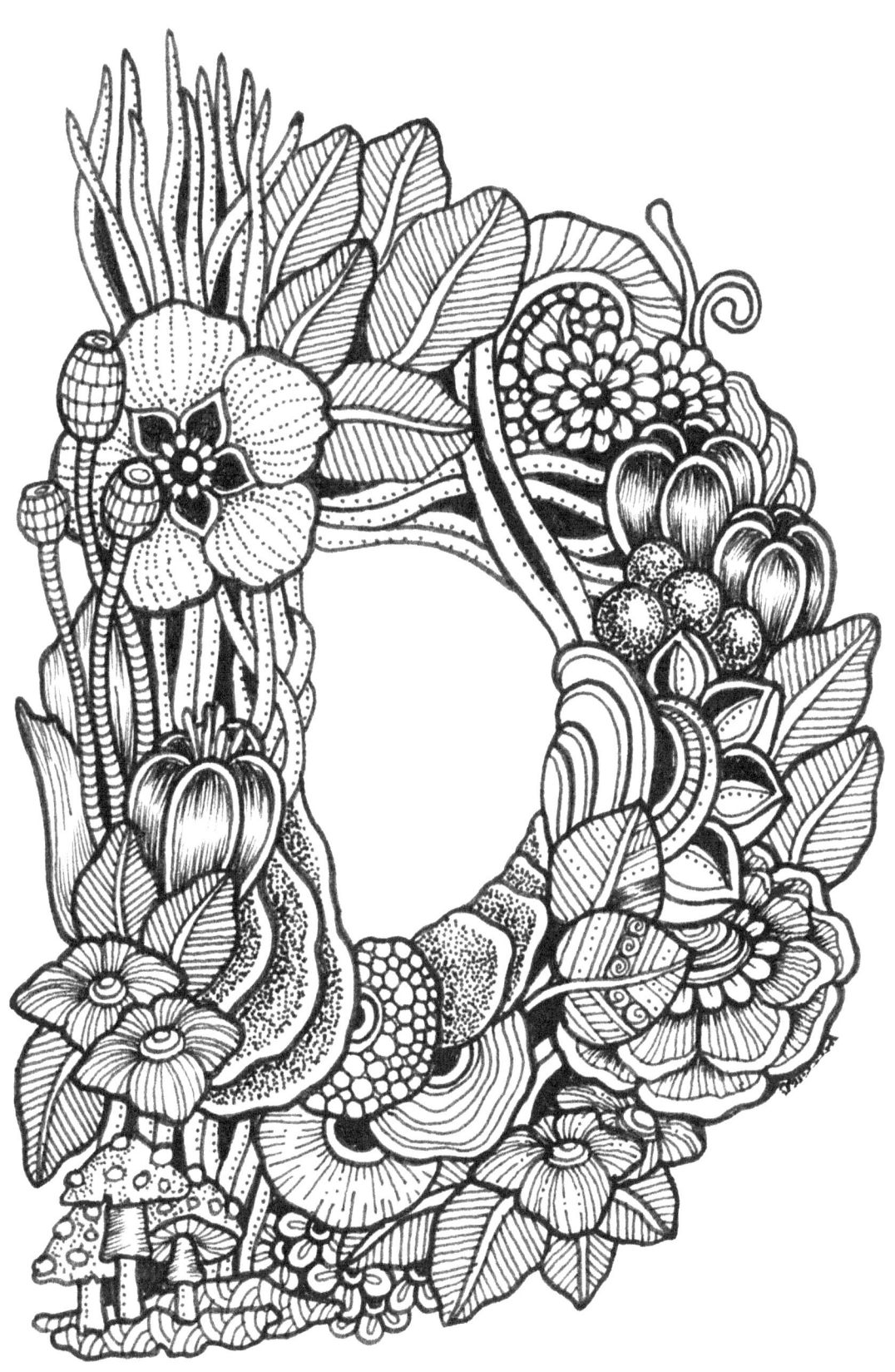

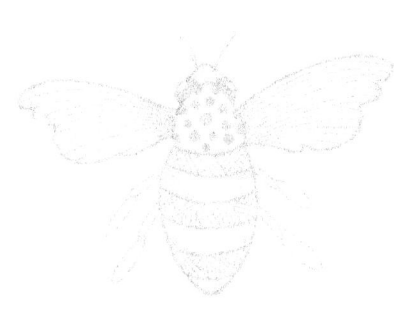

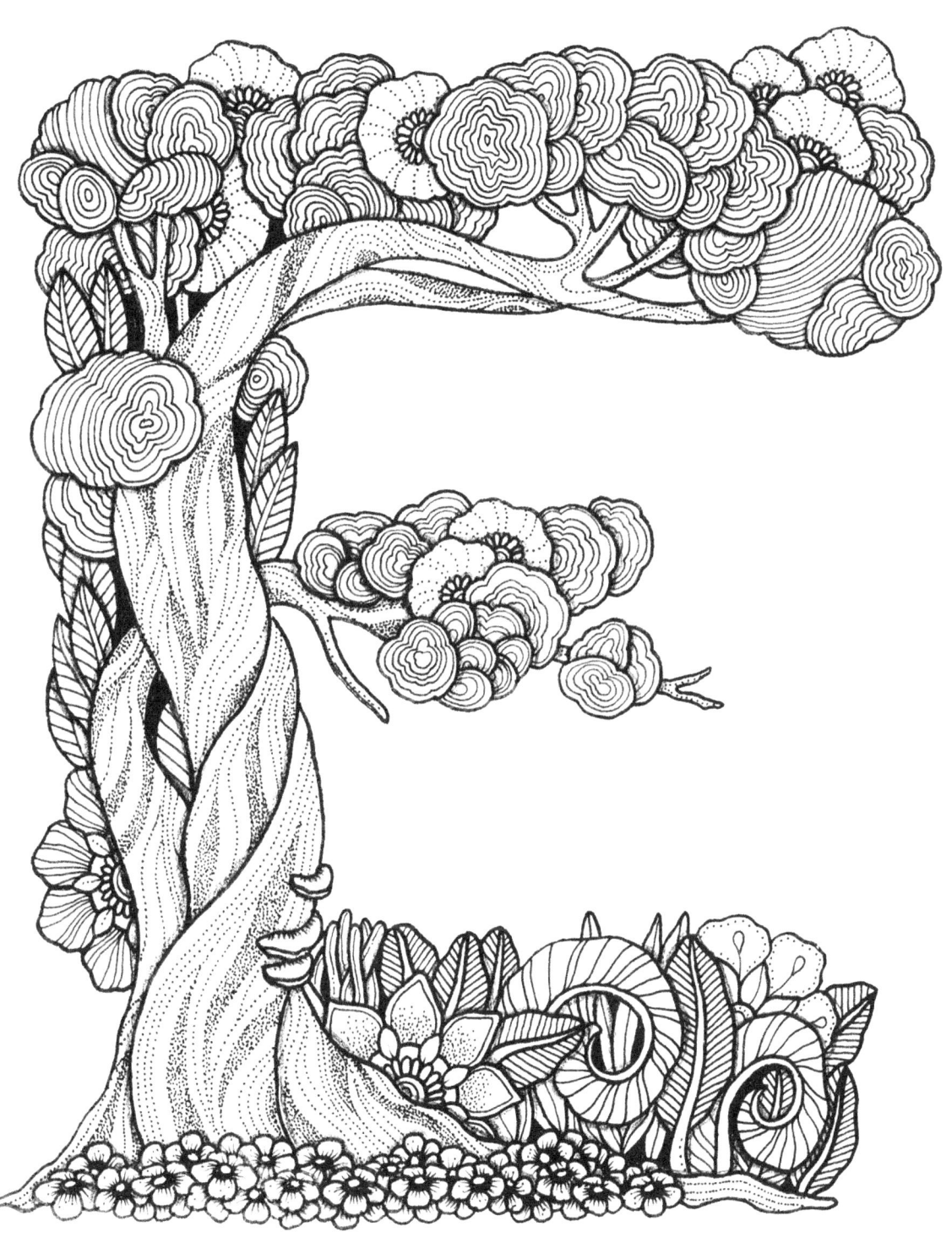

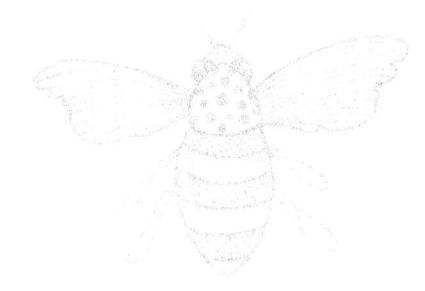

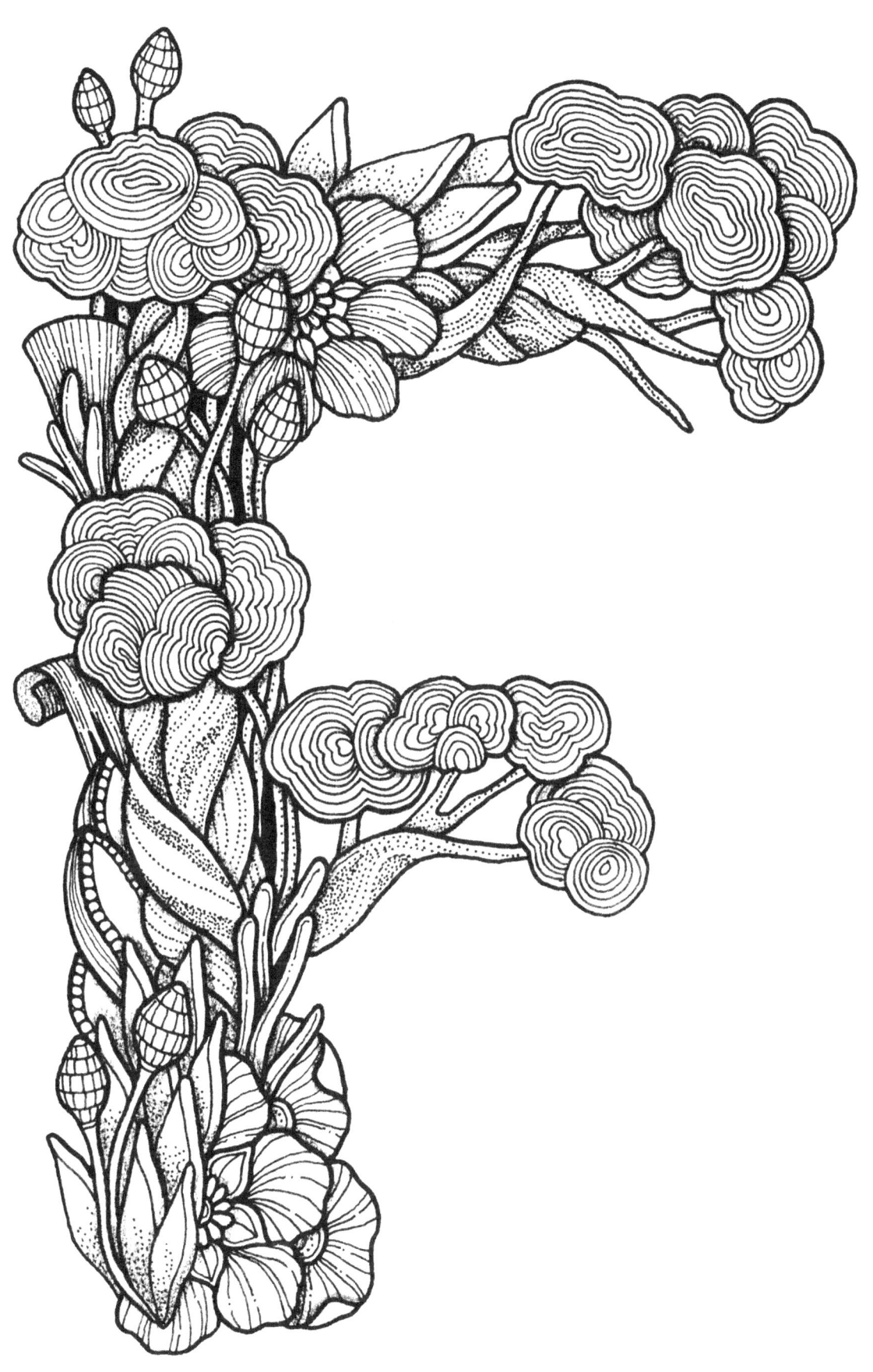

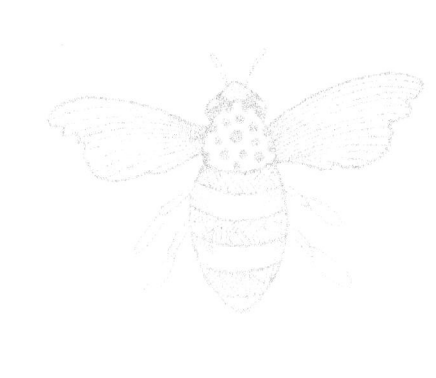

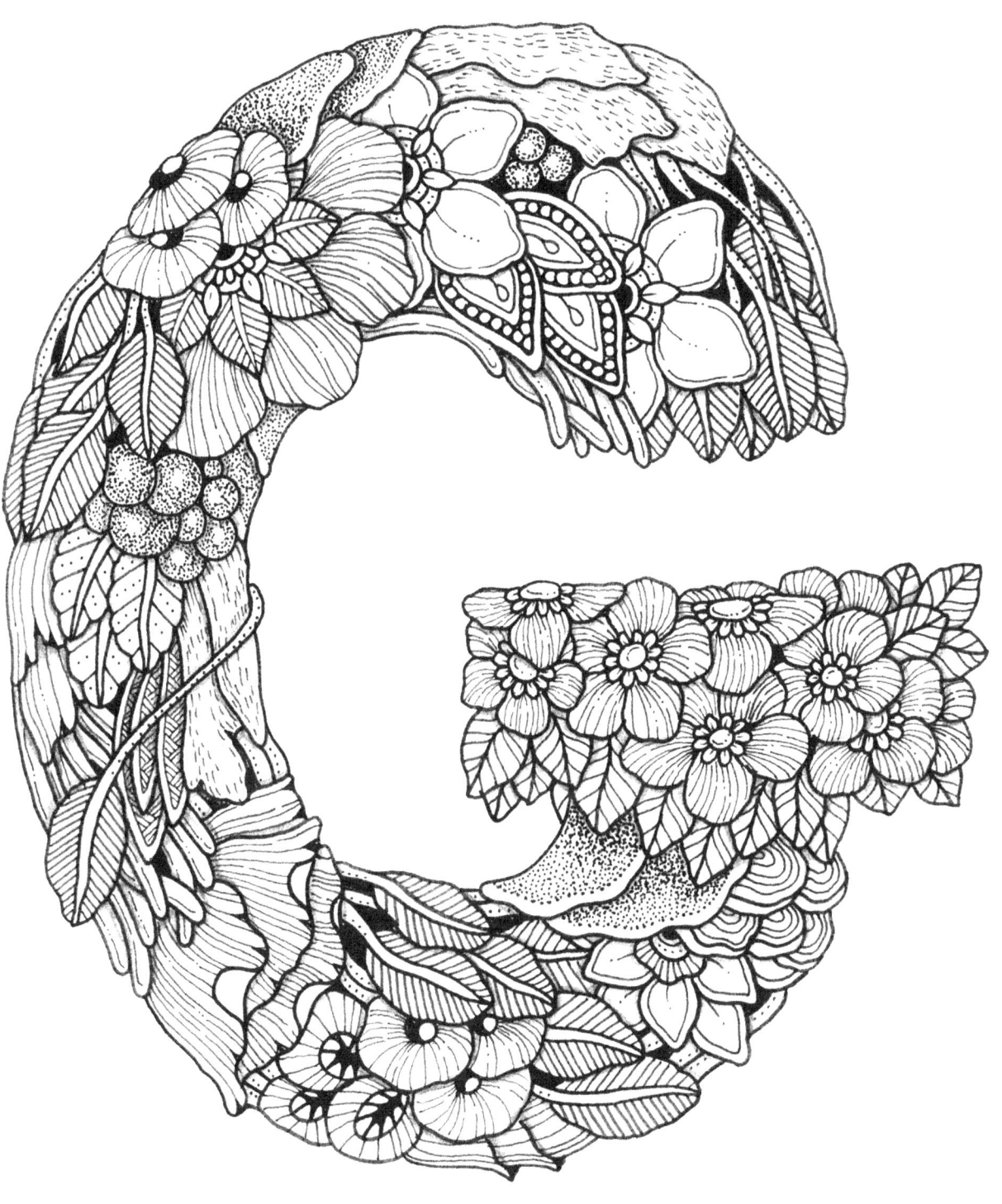

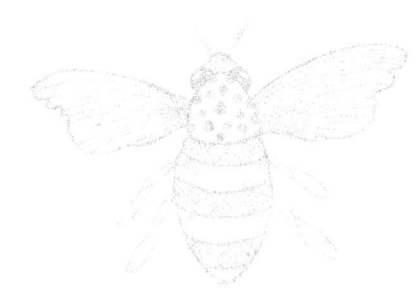

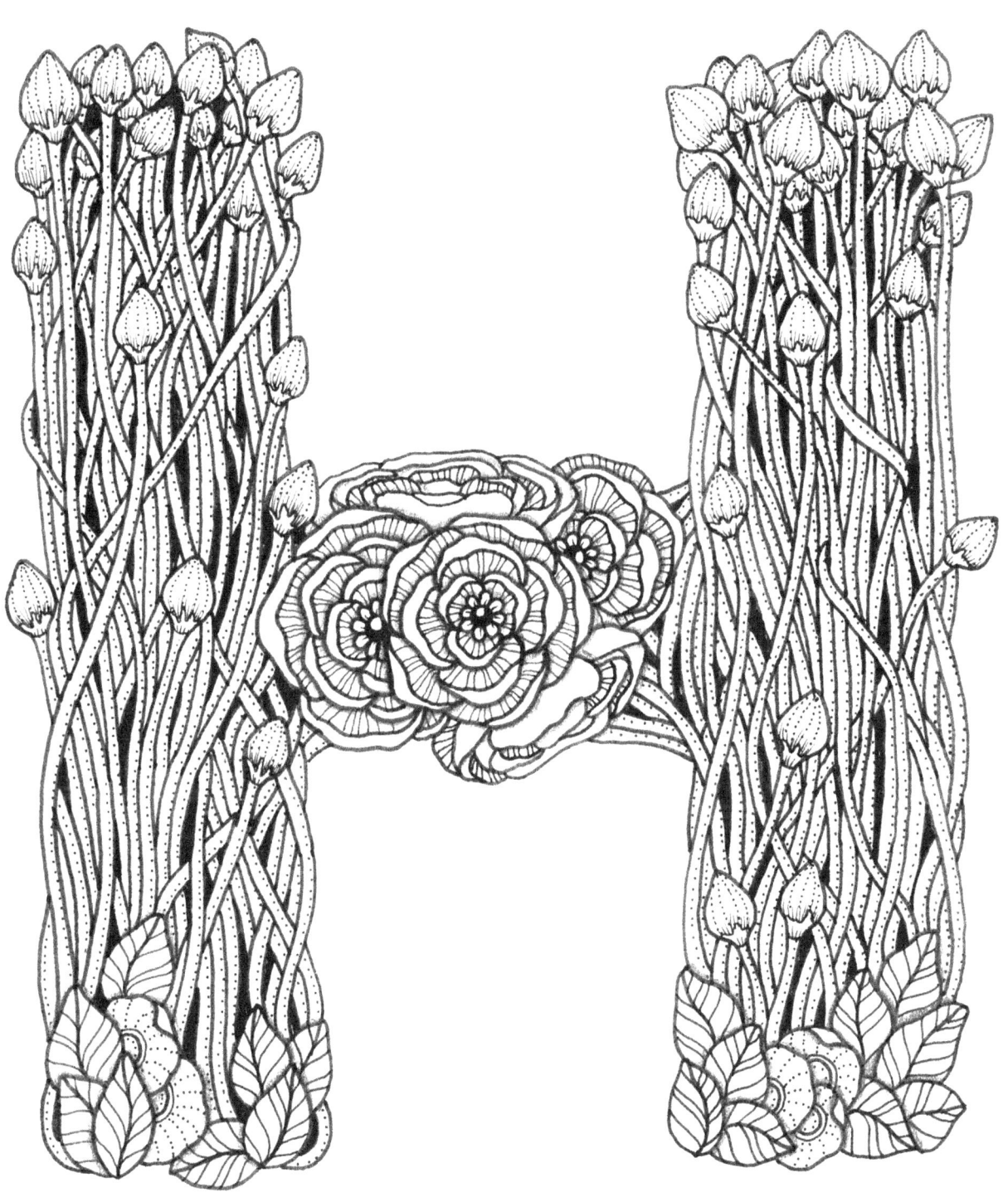

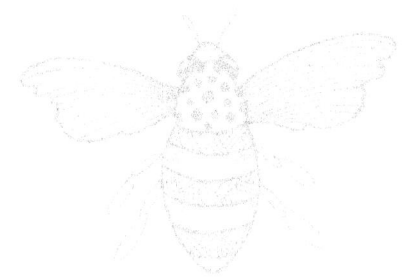

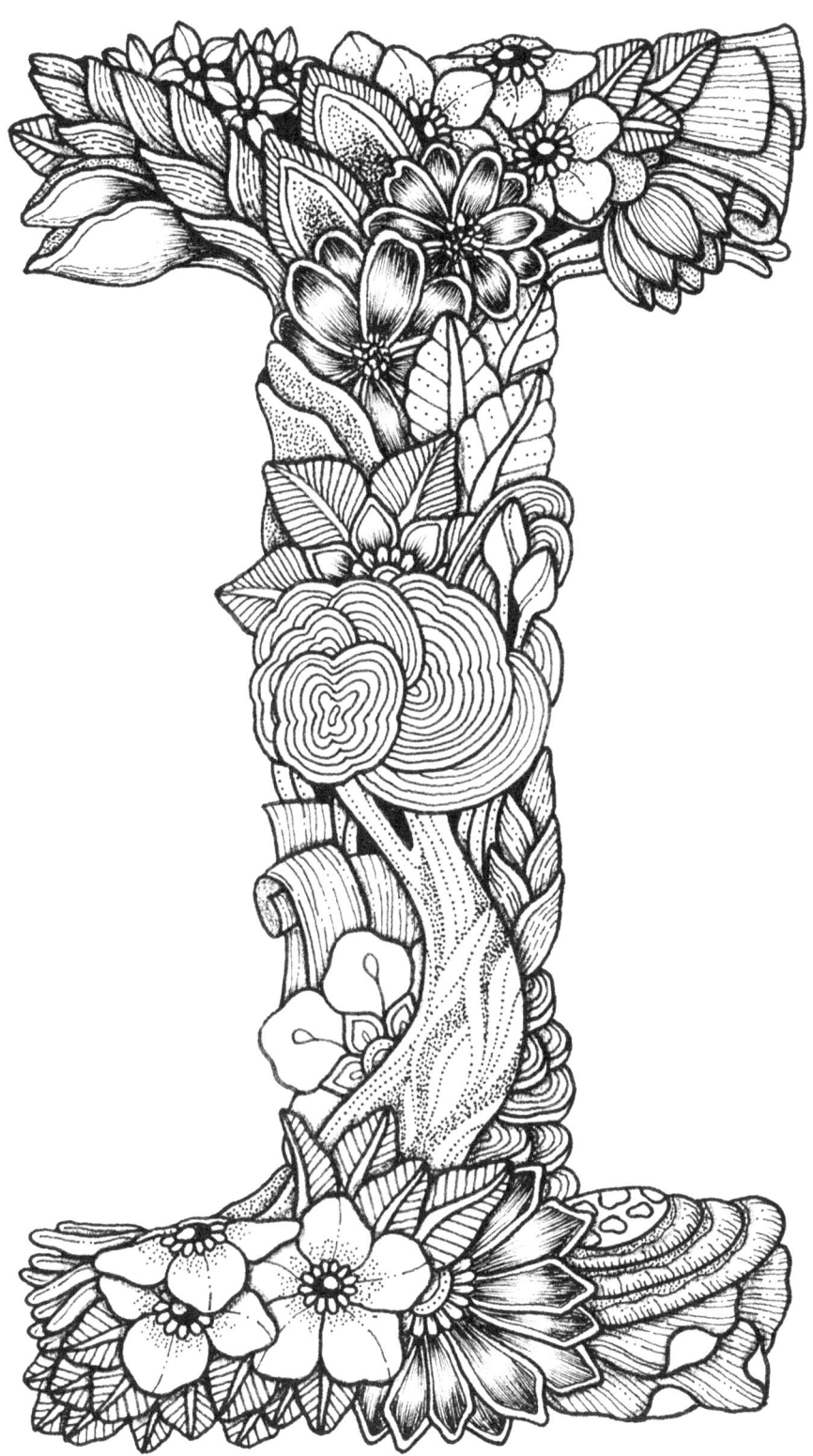

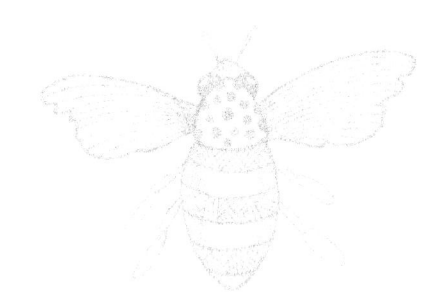

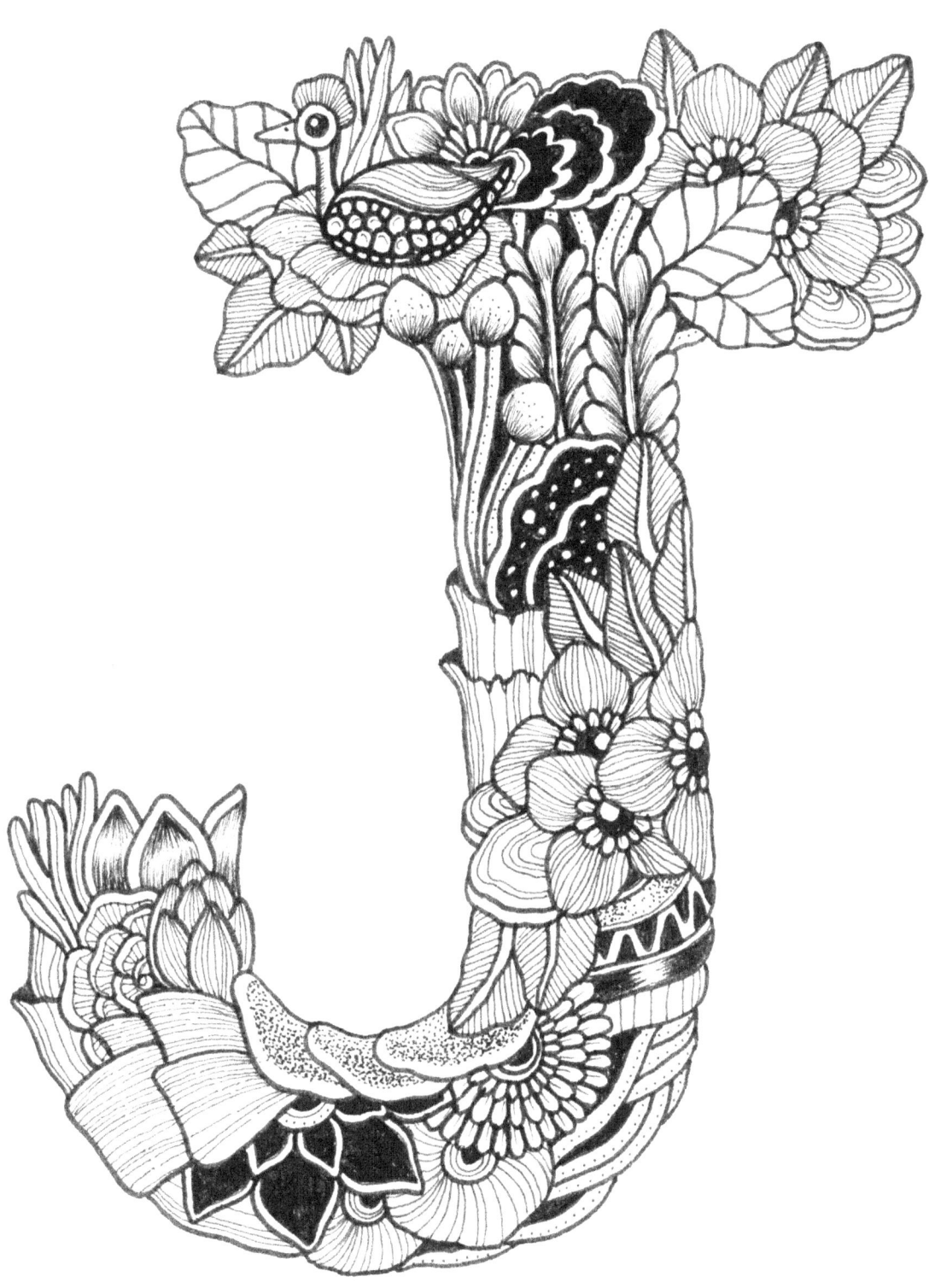

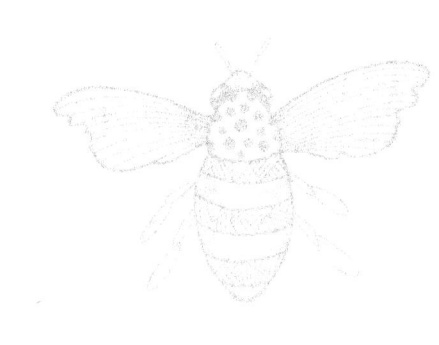

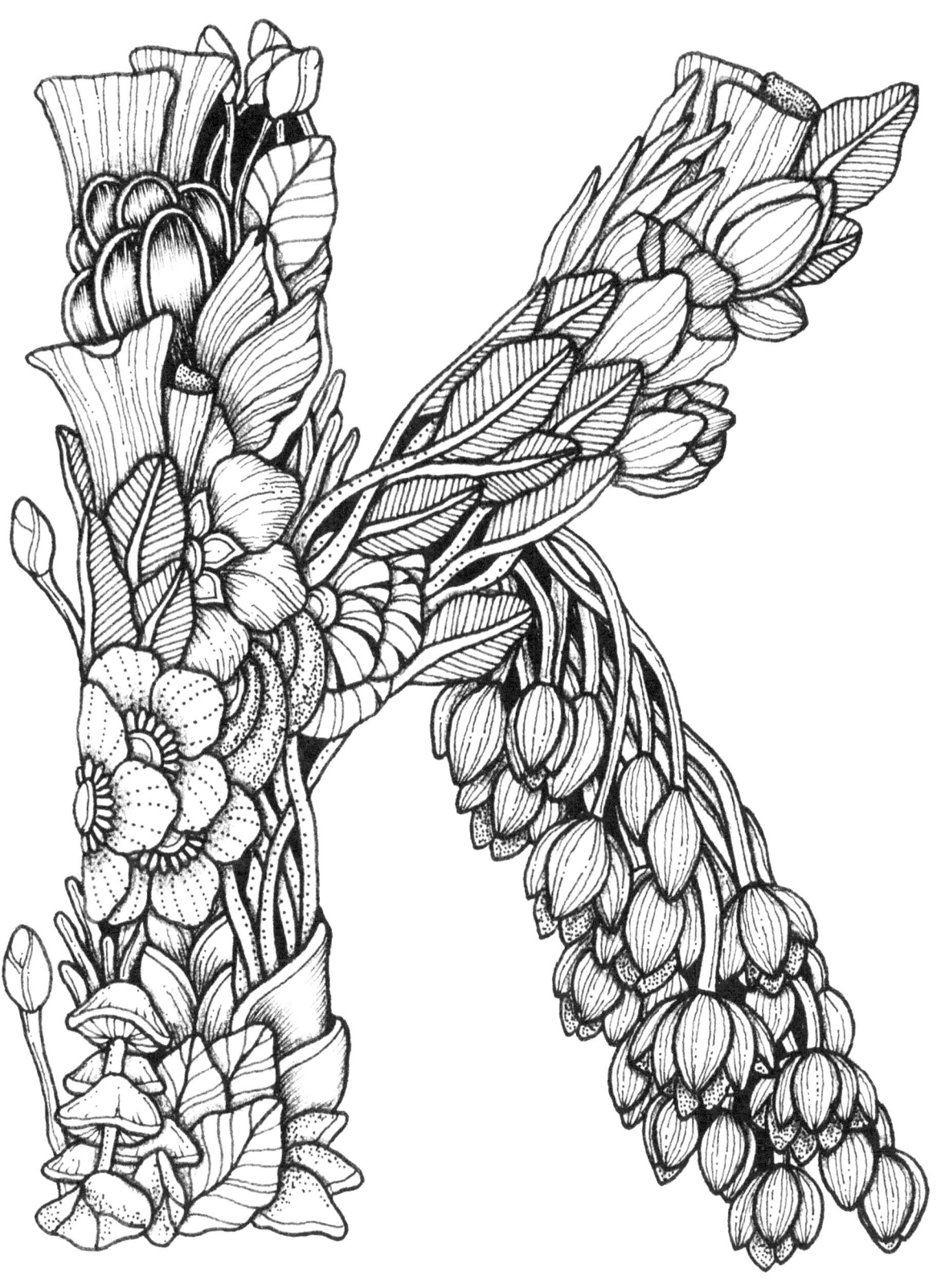

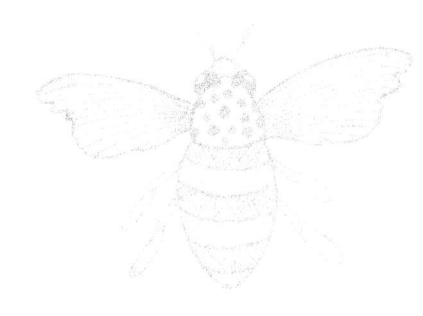

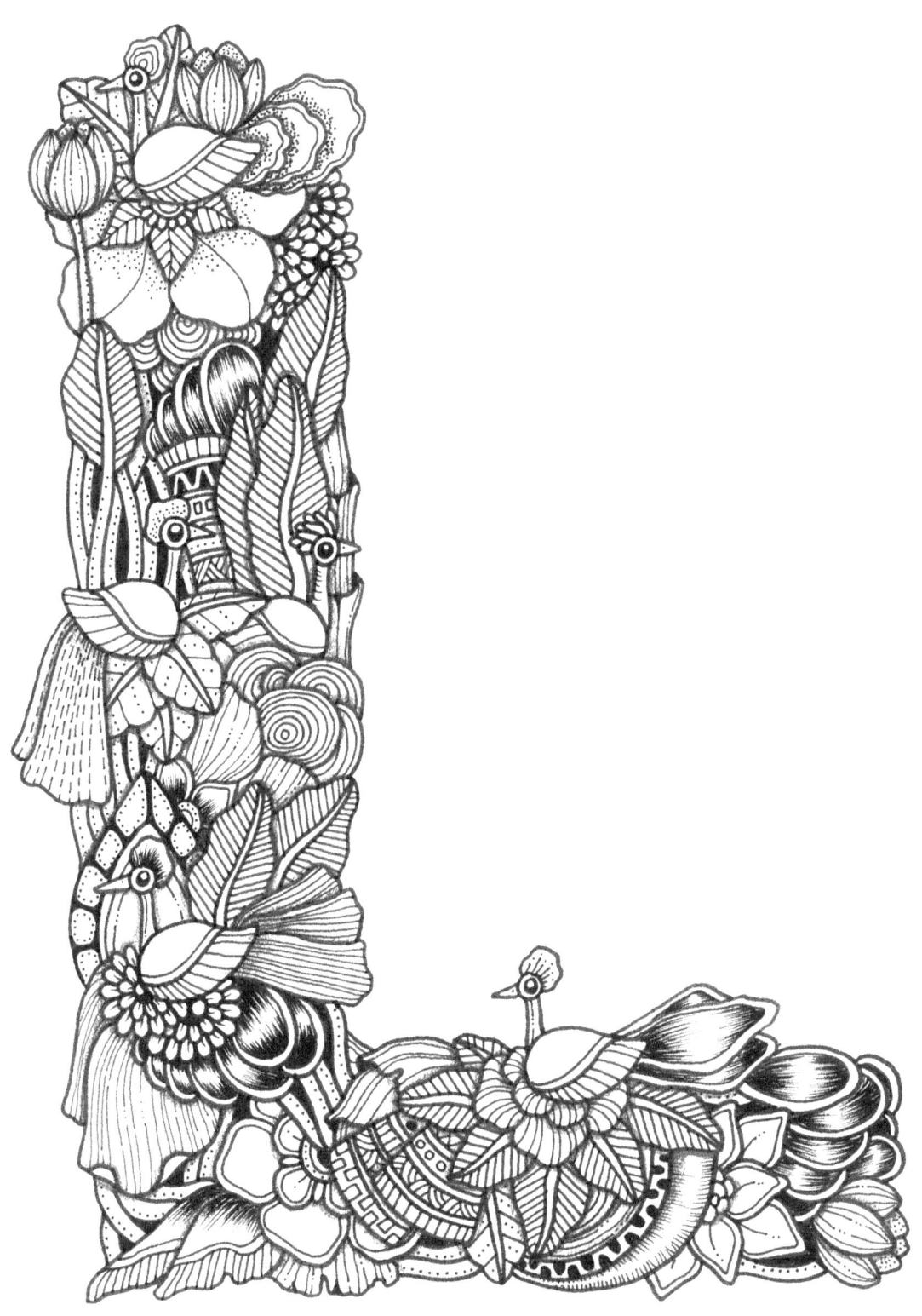

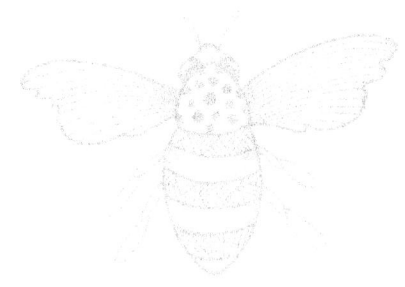

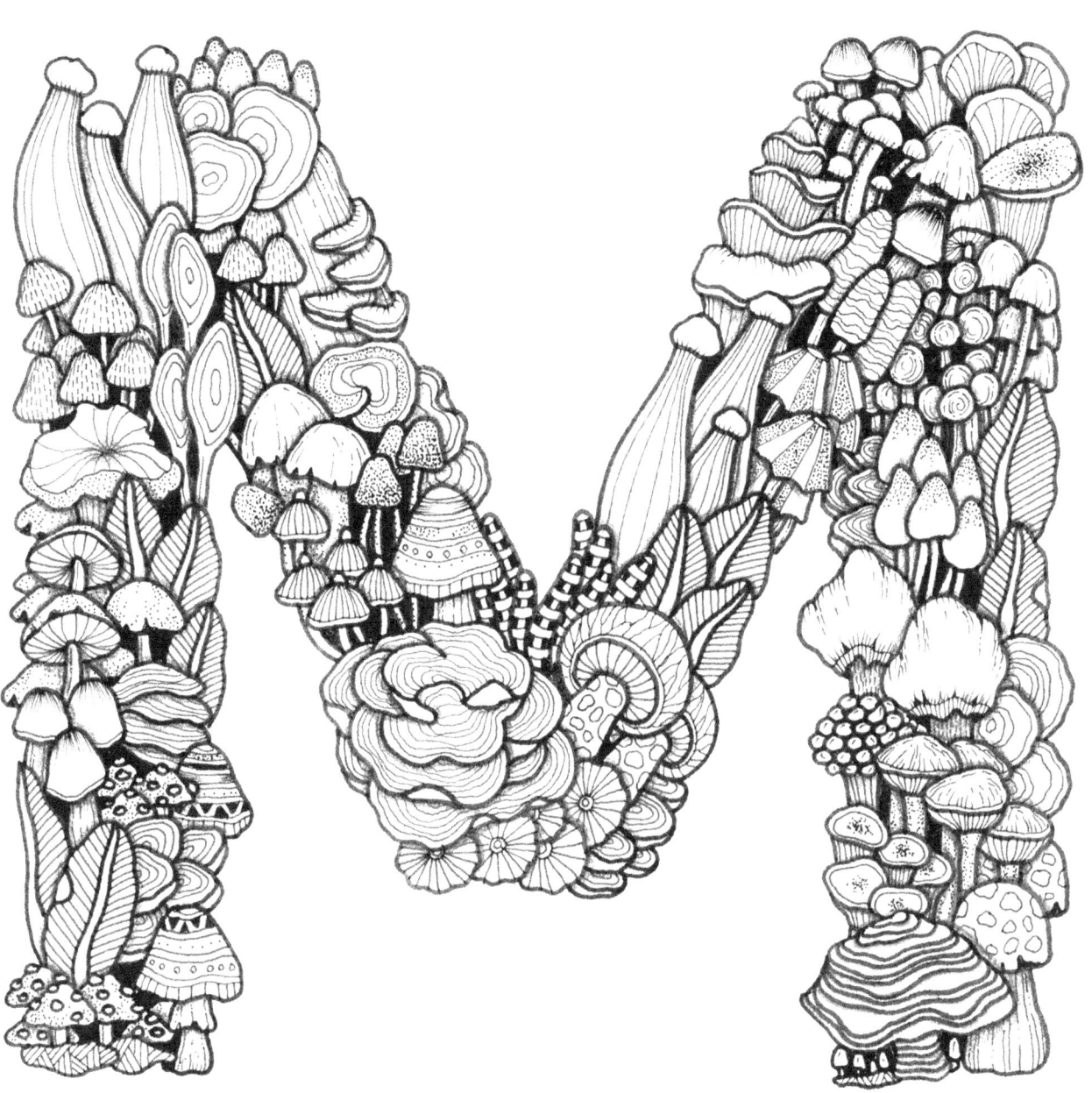

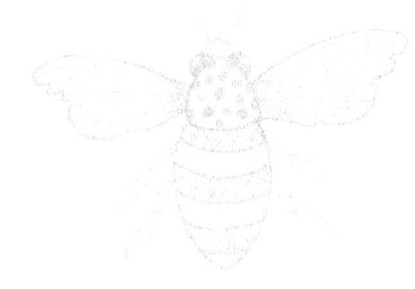

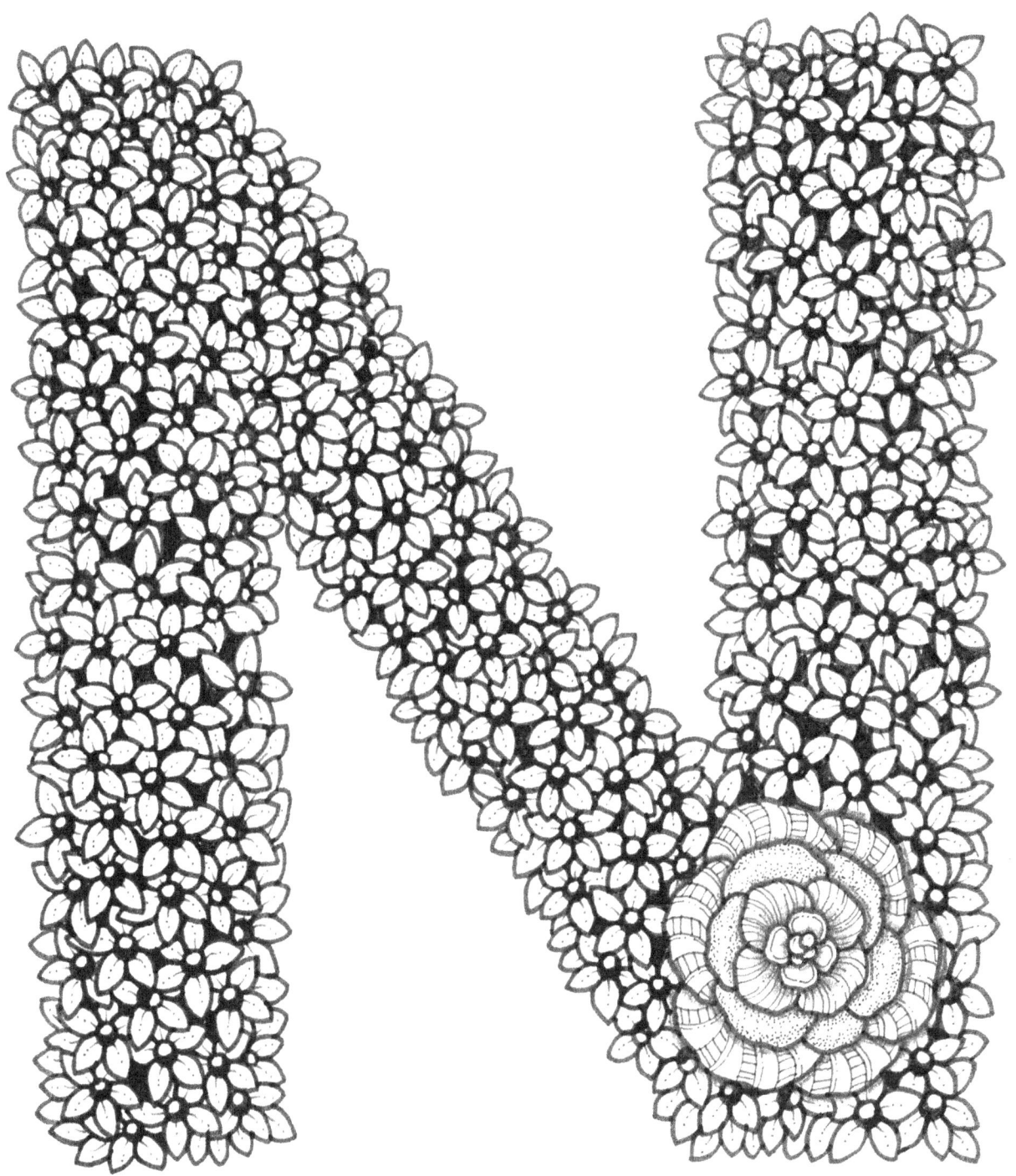

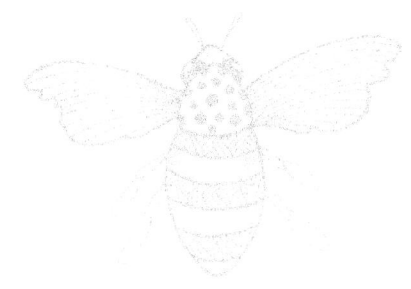

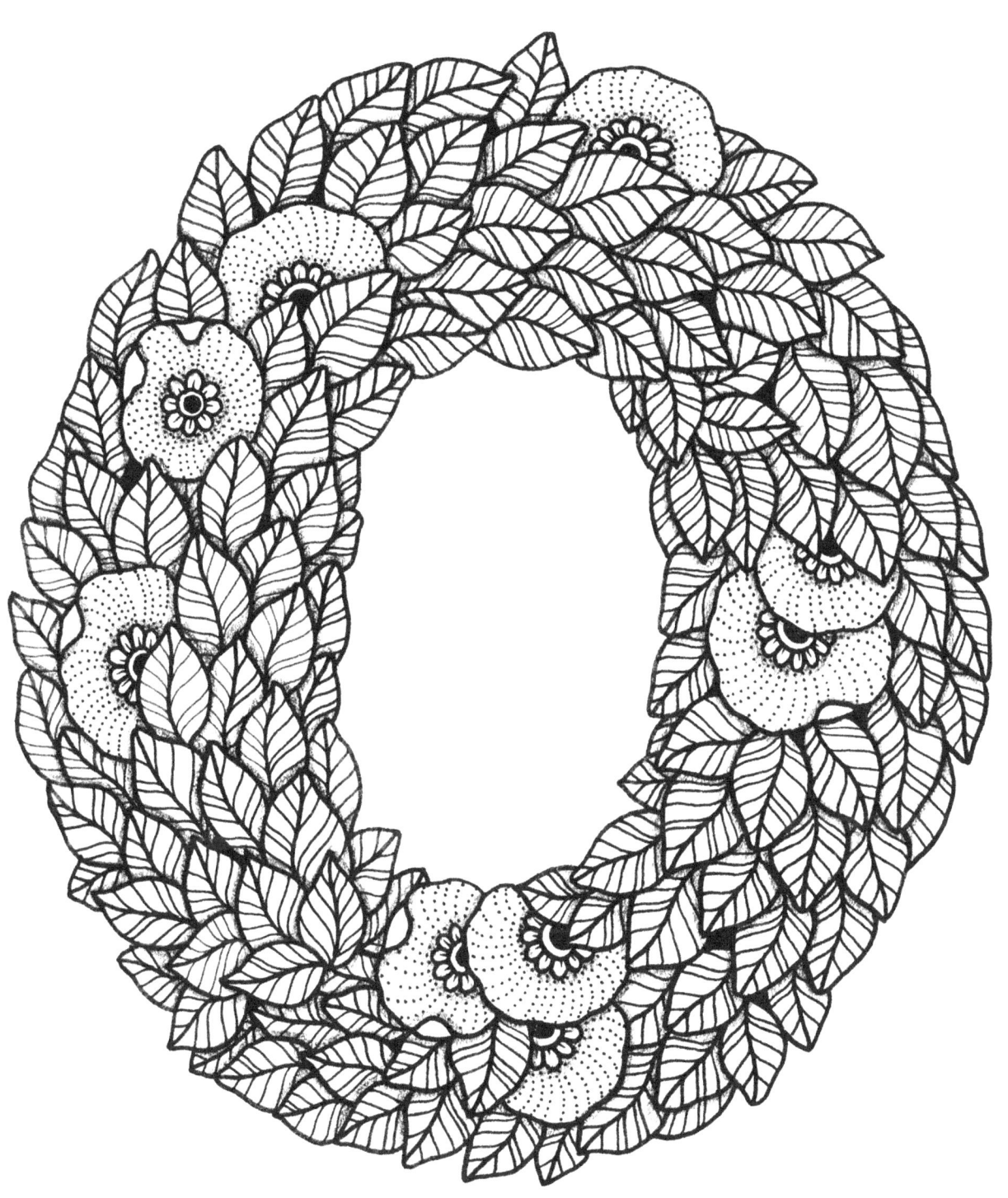

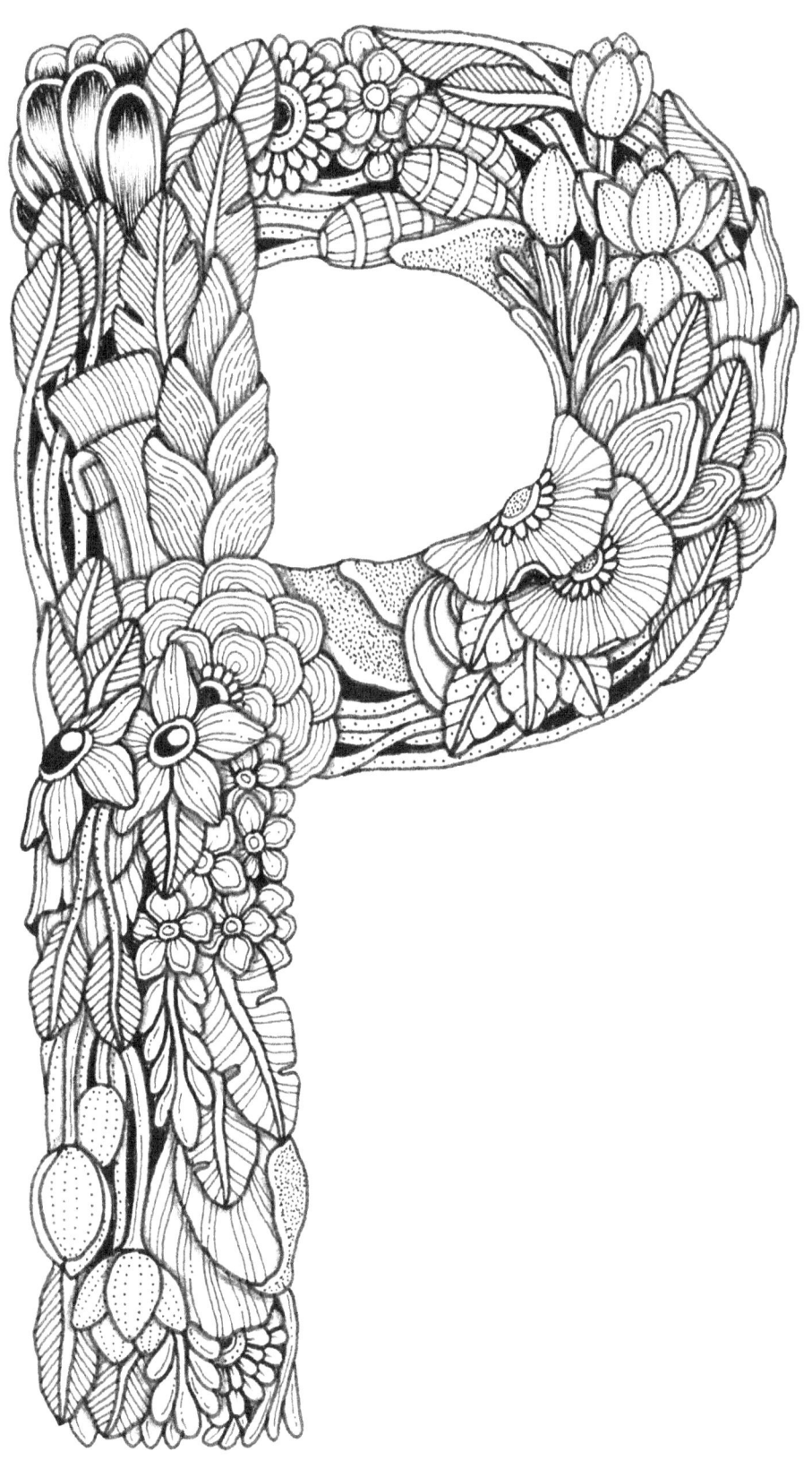

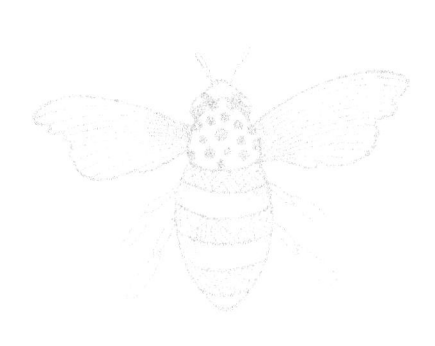

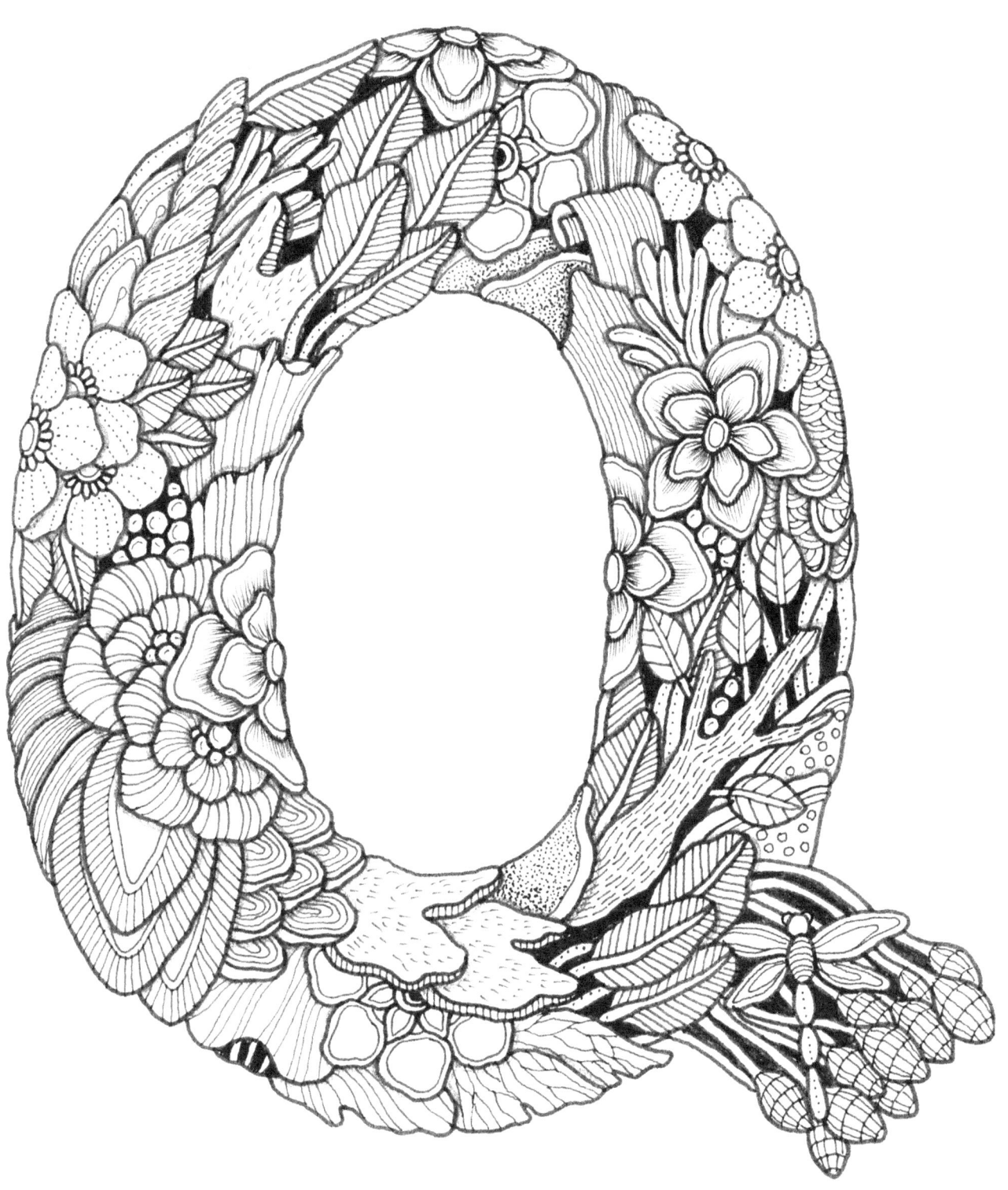

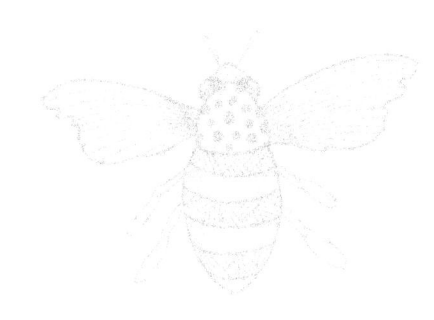

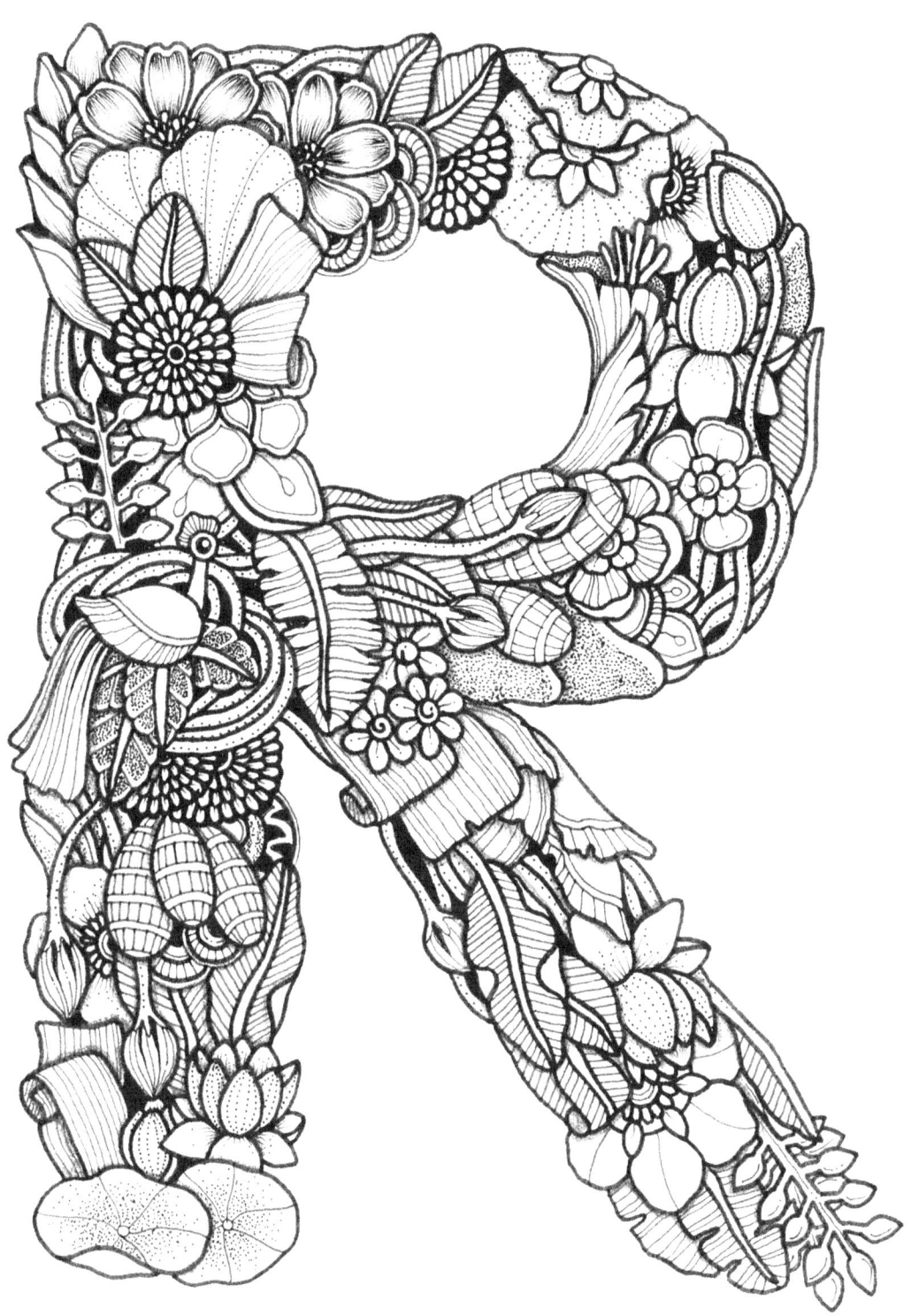

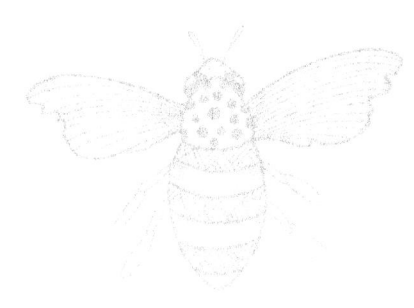

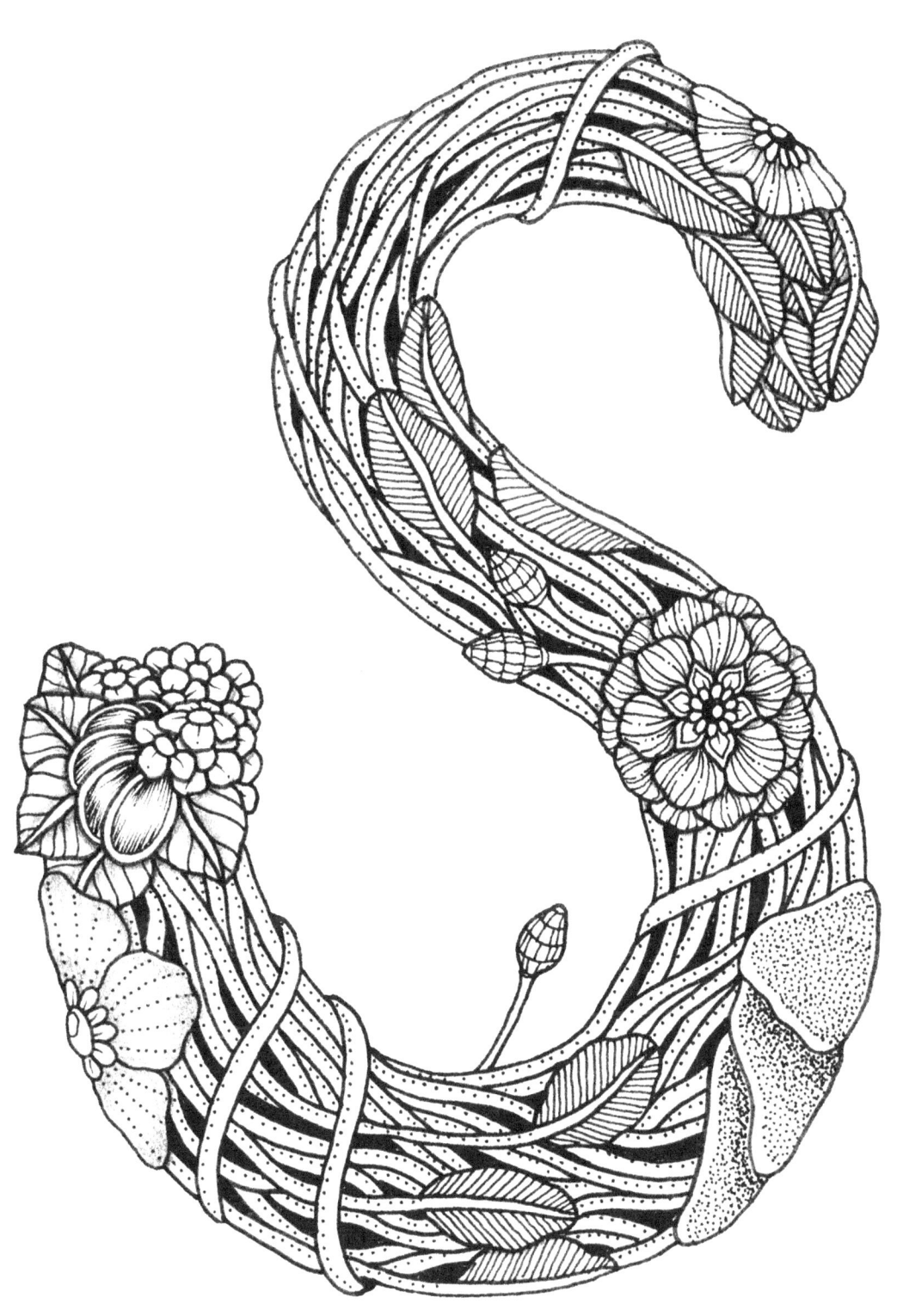

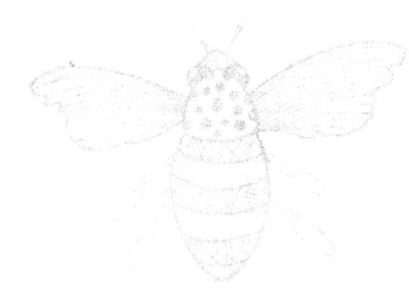

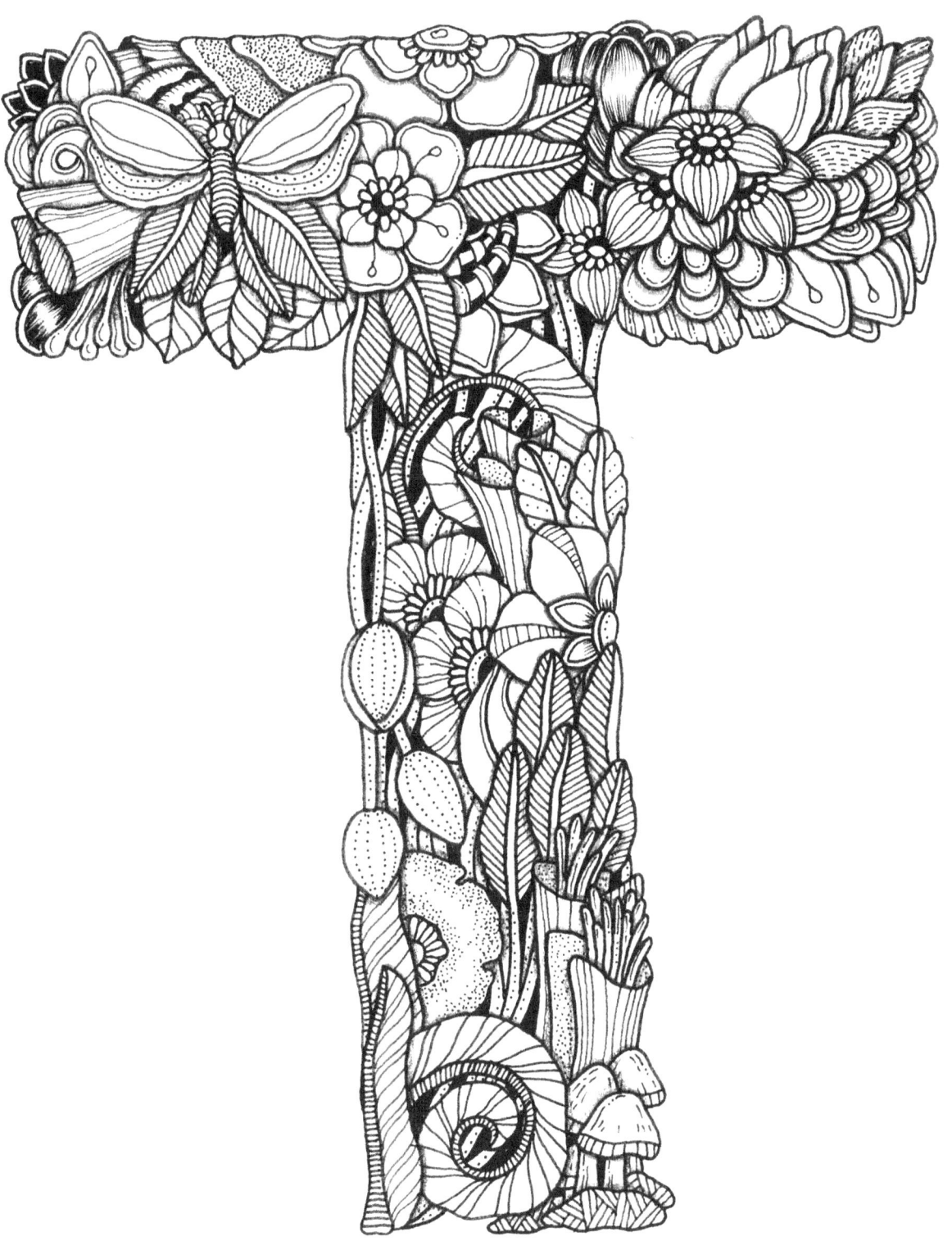

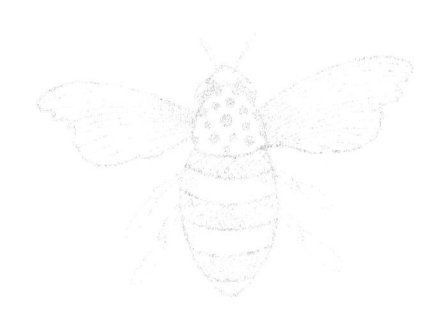

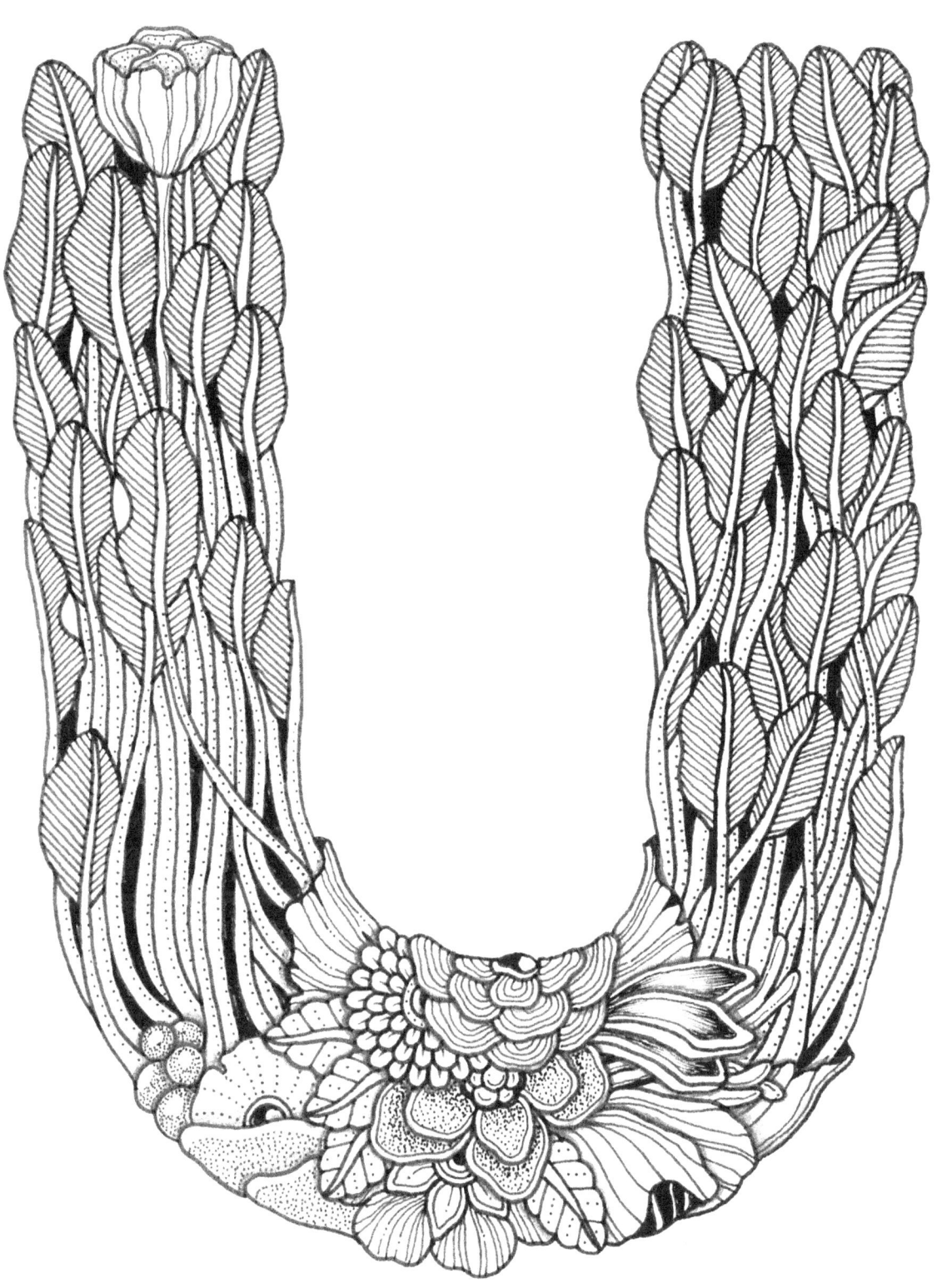

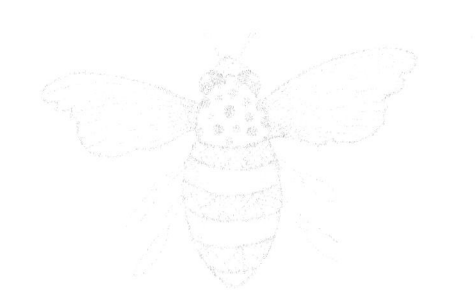

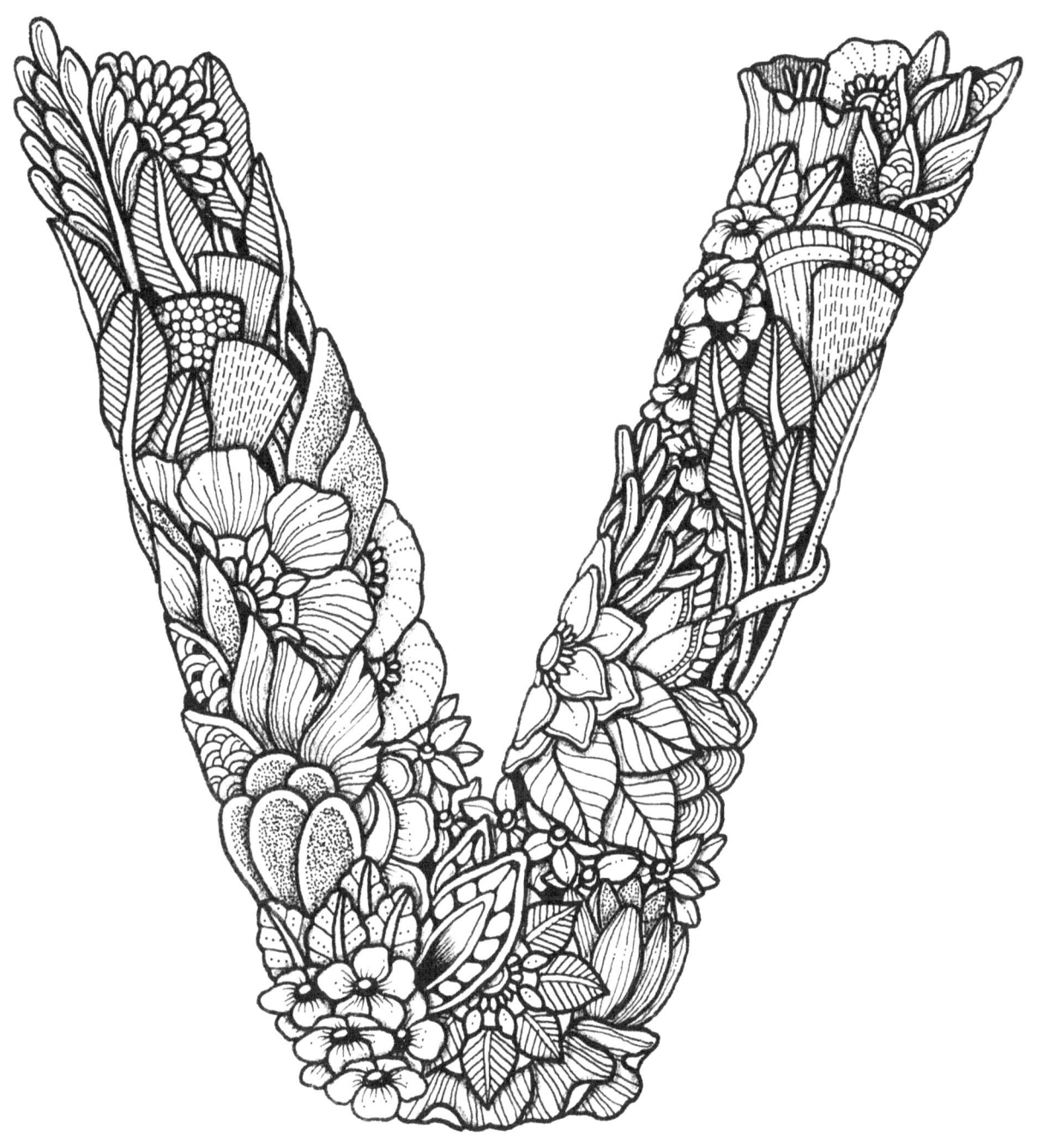

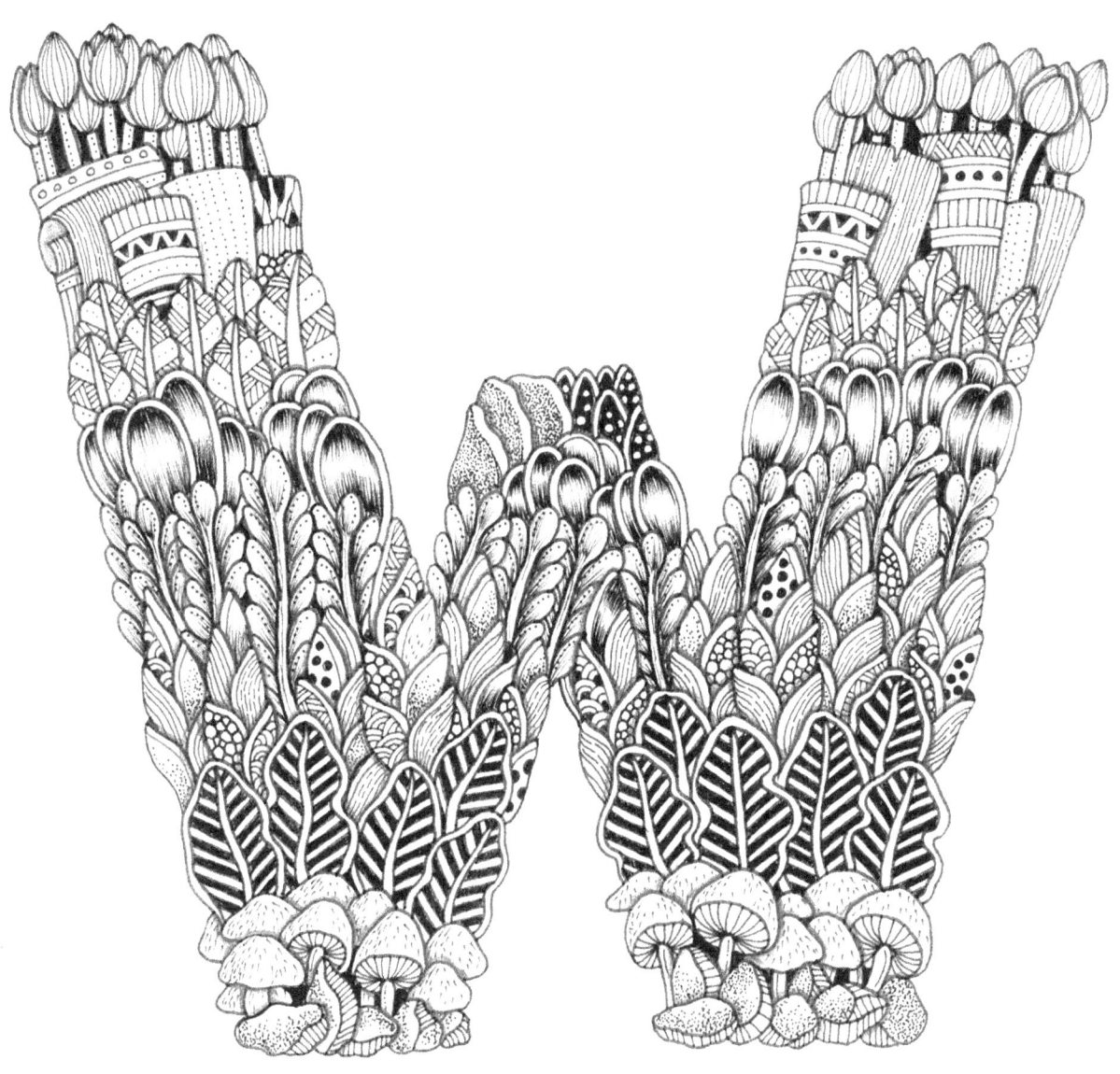

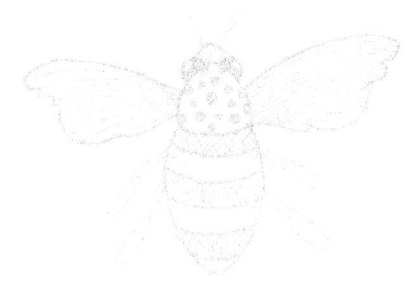

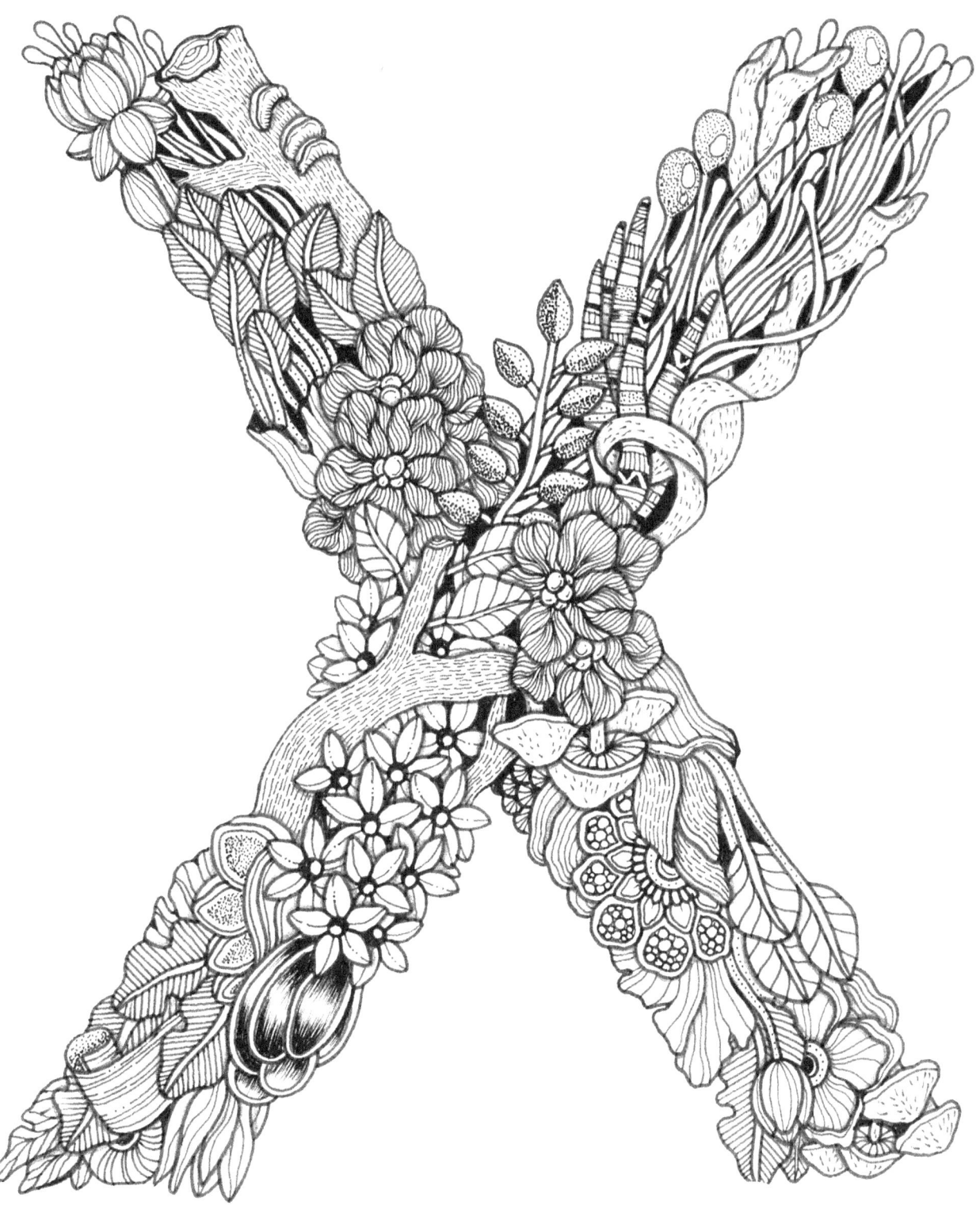

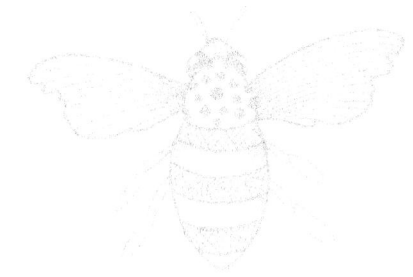

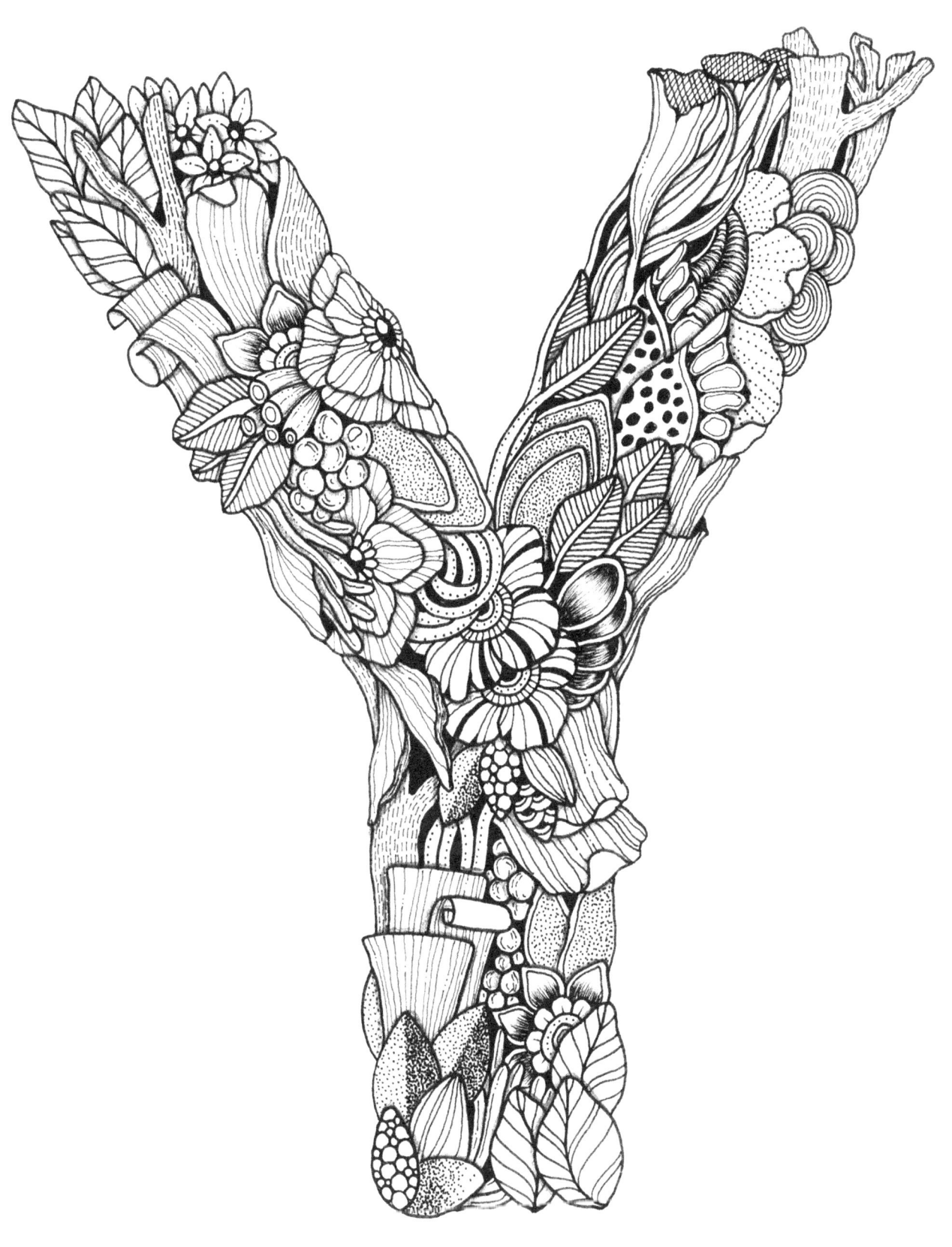

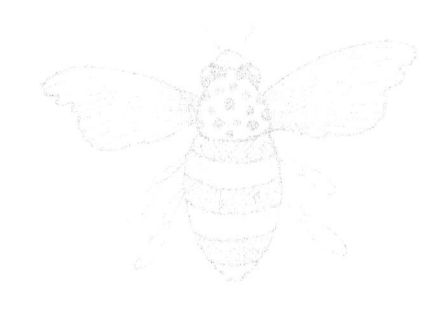

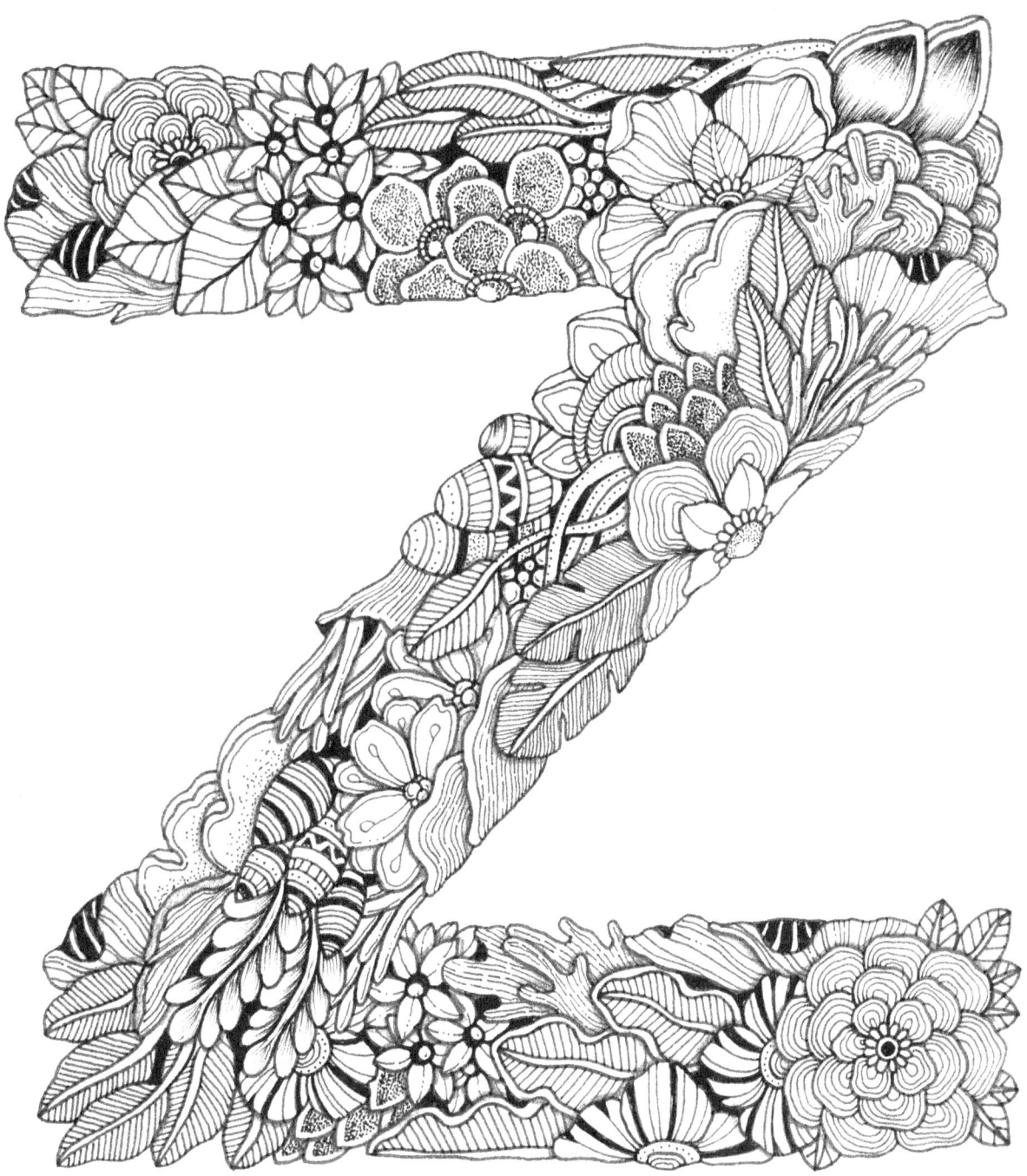

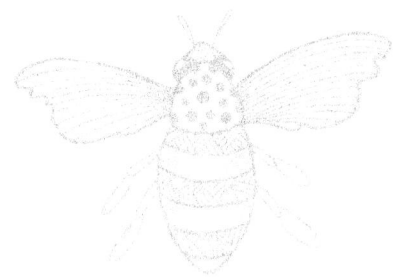